EMAILS

From
Heaven

Your Spiritual Guide to Life

Maya Knight

Maya Knight's

EMAILS
From
Heaven

Written by
Maya Knight

Design and Layout
Maya Knight

Published in 2019

PO Box 179
Bulahdelah 2423 NSW Australia
maya.palmist@gmail.com

www.mayapalmist.com.au

Emails From Heaven

All Rights Reserved

Copyright © 2019 Maya Knight

Reproduction in any manner, in whole or in part,
in English or any other language, or otherwise,
without the written permission of the copyright holder is
prohibited.

First Printing 2019

ISBN: 978-0-6485538-0-9

Acknowledgements

Certain people enter your life and because of them, you change and your life takes on new meaning and greater definition and depth.

As I look back on my life, I have been challenged and blessed by so many people and situations and I wish to give thanks for the impact, big and small, that all of you have had in shaping me and helping me to grow.

I am especially grateful for the 'EMAILS FROM HEAVEN' that I have received and I'm reminded of a Chinese Proverb:

"When someone shares something of value with you and you benefit from it, you have a moral obligation to share it with others."

To have this book in print has been a collective effort and as such I offer my sincere thanks to Russell Sturgess who, unbeknown to him was the instigator of my first 'Email from Heaven.'

To my wonderful children, Kristy and Steven – You were my greatest teachers, especially on the subject of unconditional love.

To Trevor, my husband, my best friend, and my soul mate – You saw the spark and ignited and inflamed me to be all that I can be. Thank you for your deep love and support.

I am so proud of all we've created.

Thank You.

Dedication

I dedicate this book to you, Mum.
Whenever I think of you,
I do so with the deepest sense of gratitude.
Thank you for your sacrifices, your commitment
As well as your faith in me to become all I am.
Thank you mostly for teaching me
That through all the trials of life,
Love (in all its forms) is what we must hold most dear,
Because it is love that always sustains us
And brings us our greatest joy.

Your capacity to love and to love life is my inspiration.

You are my guiding light.
You are My Night Star.

Contents

A Successful Life	Page 1
Abundance	Page 3
Be Patient	Page 5
Be a Star	Page 6
Be a Seeker of The Truth	Page 9
Becoming	Page 11
Be True to You	Page 13
Change	Page 17
Children	Page 20
Choosing Your Path	Page 25
Confidence	Page 27
Creating a Peaceful Life	Page 29
Dissatisfaction	Page 32
Expectations	Page 34

Explore Your True Potential	Page 36
Faith, Hope and Charity	Page 40
Finding Fulfilment	Page 43
Finding Life's Purpose	Page 46
Follow Your Dreams	Page 49
Fulfil Your Heart	Page 51
Grief	Page 53
Happiness	Page 56
Heart, Mind and Soul	Page 60
Inspiration	Page 62
It's Your Choice	Page 66
Integrity	Page 71
Joy	Page 72
Just Be You	Page73
Knowing Your Self	Page 76
Learning To Love	Page 80

Learn To Fly	Page 85
Let Go and Let God	Page 87
Love	Page 90
Making Your Life Count	Page 92
Marriage	Page 97
Meditation	Page 101
Old Age	Page 105
Reaching Your True Potential	Page 107
Reality	Page 110
Relationships	Page 112
Relationships 101	Page 116
Rise Above Yourself	Page 121
Romance	Page 124
Self Esteem	Page 127
Self Love	Page 128
Self Worth	Page 130

Success In Life	Page 135
The Journey of Life	Page 136
The Meaning of Life	Page 141
The Train Of Life	Page 148
Thoughts	Page 151
Time	Page 157
Trust Yourself	Page 162
Truth	Page 165
Unity	Page 169
Use Your Gifts	Page 173
Your Garden	Page 175
Your Life Is In Your Hands	Page 176
Your Time On Earth	Page 179
To Be Remembered	Page 182
Conclusion	Page 184

Author's Note

I want to introduce you to this book, a book I'm very proud of . . . a book that hasn't actually been written *by* me, but *through* me.

So where did it come from? 'I really don't know!'

I know that sounds strange, but that's the truth of it. I've asked the question many times and the only answer I have received was this:

It is not for you to know the existence of all that is. Instead, follow the path that we are laying out in front of you.

When asked where this comes from it is clear. It comes from a place deep within your being that is 'all knowing'.

You are the bringer of the truth. You are the resting place for weary souls who need to re-commence their journey to that place of peace and love.

Do not doubt for we have given you signs and proof of our existence.

All too often, the emphasis is on 'who' the author is, rather than on the words written.

So in this instance it's the words that are important.

In fact they are so important that I have been unable to change them.

Although each chapter is complete within itself, there is a similar theme throughout . . . and that theme is 'love'.

It's about giving love.

It's about receiving love.

It's about loving yourself.

It's about being yourself.

It's about just 'being'.

It's about being the best you can be.

If I had one wish that I could grant you, it would be to really
LIVE, LOVE and LAUGH.

Enjoy every moment of your life's journey.

Make your life wonderful.

Make your life meaningful.

Be all you can be.

Do all you can do.

Mostly, love completely, honestly and unconditionally every moment of every day of this precious gift. . . . . Your Life

Changing my thinking

Changes my beliefs

Which changes my expectations

Which changes my attitude

Which changes my behavior

Which changes my performance

Which will change

My life

A Successful Life

Many are lost in their path.
They believe there is only
One path for them,
One bus to catch,
One train to ride.

Do they not see
That there are many roads
And many offshoots
Available to them?

They measure their true worth
By linear time,
By destinations reached,
Not by the adventures of the soul,
The journeys of the mind,
Or the feelings of the heart.

So let your heart beat strong and full,
Full of love and laughter and full of joy.
And let each thought be one that exults you
And raises those you are in contact with.

*Let each beat of your heart be in step
With your true purpose in this life.*

*The search for purpose is simple.
Know yourself.
Be yourself.
Speak only with love.
Sense only good.
And listen to your soul.
Be still in times of doubt.
Act steadfastly in times of need.
Create.
Walk forward.
Stand tall and proud.
Let your doubts keep you humble.
Let your pride keep you noble.
Let your love keep you strong.
Let others sustain you.
Let your friends encourage you.
Let the hand of God touch you.
Let age shape you.*

*And never fear what lies ahead,
For what lies within expressed with love
Will see you though all turbulence
And hard times.*

Abundance

*Abundance is yours
If you close your mind
And open your heart instead.*

Lift your eyes up.

*Do not look down for in looking down
You will only see the dust
That you have left,
Instead of the sunlight
That is paving your way.*

*Look not at the shadows of your life.
Shadows are not to be feared
Because they are only the remainders
Of your illuminations.*

*For everything there is a component of waste.
Know what you must eliminate
And you will be able to go forth
Much more quickly.*

It is too easy to get bogged down
In unnecessary clutter and dealings.
Open your eyes and you will see
That the way is clear to you.

You will find that each day
Will bring its own gifts.

Be methodical but not plodding.
Be light with your words
And be light with your thoughts.

In doing this, your steps
Will be less forced
And freedom will become your mantra.

Always choose deliberately
With carefree precision
The path you know
You must take.

Surround yourself with vivid colours
Of each new dawn,
And always arm yourself
With vitality and hope.

Be Patient

In this 'immediate' society,
You are losing the ability to dream
And to experience that joyous sense
Of expectation and waiting.

You must all find the way to re-create this,
To once again give root to the essence that exists
In each one of you.

You must find your core,
Open your husk
And accept your true spirit,
So that the process of life
May unfold unhindered.

The deck falls as it must.

Relax and enjoy all that is your life.

Trust that all you need for your highest good
Will come unto you.

Be A Star

'Throw ye not pearls before swine.'

Swine are the thoughts of negativity
That drive you away from your path.

Be clear in your intent
And know that we are there
To support and guide you.

It is all there for the asking.

Your body is your temple
And the tomb is the soul within.
Be you as the archaeologist,
Looking within for that
Which lies deep, deep within
That needs to shine without.

Be very, very clear, and be focused.

Do not stray from your path.

*Do not listen to what others say
To help guide you,
For you know within your heart
That you are to be guided by us,
And to be guided by yourself.*

*Please understand what happens
With intentions not clear,
And do not pursue paths
That lead down a dark, dark spiral.
You gain nothing with revenge.
You gain nothing with hatred.
You gain nothing with spite.*

*Send love to all those who have failed you,
And be sure that this love
Will reach a poor heart.*

*Focus your intent on the inner tombs
Of the temples you are in contact with.
And know that you are reaching
A place within a soul
That only you can reach.*

*You must clear the barriers
In order to fulfil your purpose
And shine a light for others to follow.
Then and only then
Will you be on your path.*

*Reach out to the hands that pull you up,
Not to the thumbs that hold you down.*

*Walk tall.
Speak your truth.*

*And when you speak, you must do so
With a full heart and an open mind.*

Inhale the truth and exhale the wisdom.

*As a symbol of growth, we offer to you a bud.
Plant this in your heart and feed it with love,
Nurturing, contentment, frivolity
And much, much joy.*

Bloom.

*See yourself as the shining light,
The star.*

Be a Seeker of The Truth

When you have a question,
Do not be afraid to ask.

Let the questions bubble up
And be like an unquenchable thirst.
Let your thirst for knowledge
Bring you to the well of information,
From which you drink
The nectar of eternal wisdom.

Let the words of truth
Rumble through your body.
And when you see
The glimmer of truth,
Stare it strongly in the face.

When you feel
The touch of tenderness.
Let it settle on each nerve ending,
Filling your senses with delight.

When you smell the scent of satisfaction,
Breathe it into the very depths
Of your being.

When you taste the joy of love,
Know that this gives you
But an inkling of the taste
That is yours in the hereafter.

This is the place
That you call 'Heaven'.

Heaven is the sum
Of your choices.

It is the sum of your experiences
Lived out.

You must taste it,
Touch it, see it,
Hear it and feel it,
In order for your soul
To know it.

Becoming

*There is a rhyme and there is a reason
Why every speck of dust exists.*

*From ashes to ashes and dust to dust
The wheel of life continues to spin.
The sculptor moulds from clay
What he sees in his mind's eye,
And creates a masterpiece
For others to view.*

*No one has shared his vision.
No one has followed in his steps.
But they share the outcome
And attest to seeing what he saw.*

*The inspiration is what counts.
So take the raw ideas
And put them to the sculptor
To mould into works of art.*

*You cannot do everything.
You cannot be everything.
You are 'who' and 'what' you are,*

*Use what you know of you,
And blend this with the rich qualities
You know to exist in others.*

*Find the right combination. And strive for harmony.
Blend and then blend some more.*

*Harmony exists in that
Which is appealing to the senses.
Find the raw nerve in others
That is waiting to find its fulfilment.*

*You have lived many lives;
Some empty, some full
But always with your sense
Of purpose and determination.*

*Find your sceptre and place it
In the hearts of men.*

*An acorn can lie dormant for some time
Before the husk is broken and it shoots forth
Into the solid structure it is.*

*No one looks to the seed
For comfort or for strength.*

Be True To You

Your life is made up of quarters,
And the value you put on each,
Determines the richness you reap.

You can only get in life
That, which you sow.

So sew your tapestry
To incorporate above all,
Peace, contentment and love.

Be true to yourself.
Live a true life,
A life as 'you'.

Do not be swayed to be anyone but 'you,'
Because that will be the ultimate lie.
And once you start to deny yourself,
Others will follow suit.

*You will then lose yourself
Totally in another.*

*You will spend your life
Searching for integrity and for meaning,
Because nothing will feel right in your life.*

*So stop and get to know
Who 'you' are.*

*Once lost, the road back to you
Is not an easy one.*

*There are many
Who will try to help you
On your journey,
But do not be entrapped
In their need to make you
Into someone you are not.*

*So how do you find
Your way back to you?*

*How do you discover
Who 'you' really are?*

*How do you take away
Layers upon layers of alterations
Made to your exterior veneer
That disguise the real you?*

*This is not to say that enhancement
Is not valid.*

*It is indeed a respect
For your body
That you take care of it,
And present it to others,
In its best possible light.*

*It is only when the veneer
Becomes so thick,
And the glue that
Holds 'you' together
Is man-made and not of God,
That the true essence
Of 'you' is lost.*

*So, to make your mark in life,
You must trust yourself.*

And be yourself.

You were born to be 'you'
Your parents, your siblings
And other factors in your life
Are there to mould you.

They are there to test you
And to help you
Clearly see the direction
That 'your' life is taking

Contrasts, light and shade,
Darkness and illuminations,
Are all there to enhance
The many facets you have.

The diamond miner
Must unearth the rock first.

The diamond in its raw state
Must then go through
Many hands and many processes
Before it sparkles and emits
The brightest light.

This too, is true, of you.

Change

*A mother's love comes
As water from the well of life.*

*It is rich to the soul and imparts
Blessings and joy to the embryo.
It is sustenance to the flow of life.*

*In your childhood you must learn
The lesson of acceptance;
Acceptance of the self,
And acceptance of the gifts
That are bestowed upon you
In this lifetime.*

*You might not accept
All your blessings,
For sometimes they are
Disguised in hardship.*

*They come to you in order that you
May reach deep into your soul,
For that which lies deep within.*

It is through struggles that you come
To a greater understanding of yourself.

It is through joy that
This understanding finds a voice.

You must not dwell
In the land of suffering,
For this will only lead to a life
Of desolation and hopelessness.

You must instead reach
To the tallest pinnacle of your being,
And stand at the precipice of enlightenment.

Look forward into the unknown,
Knowing with certainty
That within 'you' lies the strength
To face all that may come.

Do not fear change,
For change is the only constant
You can rely upon.

It is change that harnesses
And propels the life force within.

*It is change that keeps
The momentum to strive for more.*

Do not procrastinate.

*Instead, use the resting phase as a time
To reflect, to regroup, to sustain, and to find peace
In the laws of give and take.*

There is a direct relationship between these.

*Just as breathing requires
The exchange of opposing motions,
So too does your life rely
On opposing and contradictory
Influences and desires.*

*Clarity and certainty in all that you do,
Does not lead to fulfilment.
Instead, it leads to a lack of creativity
And a lack of faith in all that could be.*

*Take all there is on offer
And offer all there is to give.*

Give freely.

Children

*Do not look upon your children
As your property.*

*They are a blessing unto you,
So that you may grow into your heart,
Just as they grow into their bodies,
And into their own identity.*

*The reason for two people to come together
In order to procreate, is to give of their best,
And to create a unique individual
That blends from two.*

*To care for children is not a task.
It is a blessing that many
Do not appreciate.*

*Many expect that a child is there
In order that 'they' may be loved,
In order that 'they' may benefit.*

This thinking leads down a path
Of heartache and destruction,
For a child must grow into' their' own identity.

There is no magic formula
In the raising of children,
But it is of great importance
The language and inferences
That they hear.

It is rarely the words
That will do the damage.
It is the inference the child
Takes from its delivery.

Remember to raise your children.
Hold them in high esteem for they are wise
In that they have much to teach you.

Raise them to stand tall and proud
Amongst their peers.

Hold them high so that all may see
Their light radiate.

Speak with softness and gentleness,
In order to nurture their fragile souls.

See your child as the seedling about to sprout.

Too much of anything can wilt their soul.

So prepare the field to provide
Protection, safety and nurturing.

And let love be the water
That flows into and around them.

Be sure not to smother them,
For they will drown in your neediness.

Love your children as they are,
And expect their true potential to test,
Not only their own limitations,
But yours as well.

Provide boundaries,
But do not chain them to you
And do not fence them in.

*They must be able to know
The depths of their own souls,
By experiencing life in all its dimensions.*

*Sorrow is a part of living,
For it shows the soul
The opposite of peace and joy.*

*Sorrow creates a desire to find balance,
Whilst learning the art of nurturing, forgiveness
As well as unconditional love,
Not only for others,
But for yourself as well.*

*Animals are indeed the greatest teachers,
Because they are instant;
They are loyal;
They are consistent;
And they protect the soul.*

*Animals bear no malice,
Nor do they hold resentments
Nor false judgements.*

*These destroy the joys of life,
And plant seeds of doubt
On an impressionable mind.*

See your children with wonderment.

*Nurture their bodies and
Harness and challenge their minds.*

*Keep them safe in your heart where your loving arms
Are never far away, to provide a warm embrace,
A gentle pat, and at times a stern reprimand.*

*Children want for nothing till we teach them
The meaning of desire.*

*When material desires become paramount,
The soul lays empty and contentment
Becomes as evasive and elusive
As the butterfly.*

Enjoy the things life has to offer.

*Cherish all that is given freely in
God's wondrous garden.*

Choosing Your Path

It's not really in your best interest
To plan your life too much,
Because you miss so much
When you negate challenges
And choose security instead.

The path should always be just that,
A path, a short journey that leads you
To the various roads of your life:
The road to success, happiness and love.

All these paths intertwine
To reach the ultimate road,
The road to truth, integrity and meaning.

Choose alternate paths often.
Reach for self-enlightenment.
Live a life that is just and full.

Righteousness is being right in our God's eyes,
That entity within ourselves that is pure,
That is whole and that asks for nothing,
But encompasses all.

*Religion is often people's way
Of bringing their righteousness outward
For all to see and proclaim
And give homage to.*

*You must instead let it radiate out
From a soul that can only
Give out love and compassion,
And thereby give unity to a world
That looks to divide and conquer.*

Religion in itself is not wrong.

*It is the purity of all you worship
That is open for debate.*

*Be as the rose, and allow yourself time
To grow and to bloom.*

*And know that even as a rose dies,
It will leave its mark in the memories of men,
And as a carpet for those
Whose footsteps follow on afterwards.*

Confidence

Confidence comes when the 'you'
That you think you are,
Meets up with the 'you' that
You want to be.

For most of you,
This is an enormous leap.

The green of envy is upon them
As they look at others
They wish to emulate.

This is the problem,
For you can only be yourself,
And when you try to be someone else,
You will fall flat, and all too often
Make a fool of yourself.

You are born on this earth
In your human form
To totally experience
This world as 'you',

*When you think more
On the joy of life,
You will experience greater
Happiness and fulfilment,
For you will be living
A life in true harmony.*

*Confidence is that
Big leap of faith
That says: 'I am 'me'
And I like 'me'!'*

'I am unique!'

*'There's no one
Better suited to being 'me',
Than me!'*

*'Sorry, but no one
Has the thoughts,
Heart and soul
To fill the shoes
I'm going to dance
The rest of my life in.'*

Creating A Peaceful Life

You cannot be at peace
When you are at odds with yourself.

This 'oddness' shows in the imbalance
Of your emotions and your behaviour.

You must strive for congruency.
You must learn to set
Your roots in fertile soil,
So that you may grow resilient,
Pliable and yielding.

You must give voice to your
Own thoughts and your own ideas.

Others may not agree,
But this is not to be perceived
As a negative thing.

It is through differences
That ideas develop and ideals
Are formed and take shape.

*This is the growth factor
Of your human soul.*

You cannot survive in isolation.

*You need nourishment
For your mind and for your soul.*

*Just as the body detests the influx of toxins,
The same is true of the mind and the soul.*

*Negativity is the toxin of the mind.
It runs through like weeds in a garden,
And can make idealism superfluous.*

*You must constantly weed out
The negative thought patterns
Before they turn to seed.*

*They must be eradicated and eliminated,
And the only way to do this,
Is to set up barriers to their procreation.*

*It is easy to take the road to negativity;
To give in to gossip, sarcasm
And criticism - constructive or otherwise.*

*All of these stem
From a lack of self worth,
And a feeling of aloneness.*

*What you need to strive for,
Is a feeling of oneness,
Not only with others,
But also with yourself.*

*Accept the multitude of discrepancies
That make up 'you'.*

*Bring all of the facets of 'you' together
In a way that brings joy to others.*

*Make peace with yourself
And create a sense of peace
All around yourself.*

*Put every one of the pieces
Of the jigsaw of 'you' together
In a way that fits your ideals
And makes your world,
Inner and outer
A better place
To live.*

Dissatisfaction

Throw away those tiny pebbles.
Squander your ill feelings to the wind,
For that is where they belong,
Not in the waters of your life,
Causing ripples of dissatisfaction.

Feeling disgruntled comes from a fear
Of confronting the obvious in you.

You must recognise how profound 'you' are.

Do not limit yourself with things
Designed to quicken your pace
That slow down your inner freedom
As well as your level of satisfaction.
Do not harbour resentment
For it will bind you needlessly.

Look again within your soul
And satisfy your heartfelt need.

Laugh more. Love more and the end result
Will be exactly as you will.

*Learn to respect yourself completely,
And have respect for the wisdom
Of all that life shows you.*

*Learn your limitations,
But continue to strengthen your spirit
By being true to your convictions.*

*Be kind in spirit and ask for nothing,
But always expect plenty.*

*Count your blessings and know
All will come to pass.*

Time is not as you perceive.

*Sow your seeds of hope, love,
Prosperity and creativity.*

Leave your mark in many ways.

*Put your trust in the master plan believing
That the way will be made clear for you
And that all that is happening now,
Is just part of God's plan for your Life's Lesson*

Expectations

*From little things,
Big things grow.*

*In order for the bud to bloom,
The life force within
Must be strong enough
To withstand the harshest
And severest of conditions.*

*The flower must burst forth
Unscathed and untouched
And be pure as it was meant to be.*

But the flowers often do not bloom.

The temperatures do not stay still.

Conditions do change.

*And what emerges is not
As was expected at times.*

*Sometimes it is the result of all
That came before.*

*The same is true
Of every human being.*

*It is in your 'being' and in your 'becoming',
That you become all that 'you' can be.*

*Does this mean then,
That destiny plays a hand?*

*Or is it that the forces within,
Were not strong enough
To combat those forces
From without?*

*Do not ever envisage
What the final outcome
Could be.*

*It is wholly dependant
On timing and on factors
Beyond your sole control.*

*It also relies on the strength
And the fortitude
Of that which lies within
Each one of you.*

Explore Your True Potential

When you are restless in your spirit,
And you do not allow your feathers
To find the wind currents
That will make you soar,
Know that it is because
You are looking down,
Instead of looking out.

You are searching for your truth,
In the inconsequentialities of life,
Instead of in the steadfastness
That abounds.

If you could only see that
It is not up to you to make the decision
As to how another views you.

It is not right nor forthcoming,
To dispense your fears onto others.
Misconceptions will never bring forth
A sense of happiness or well-being.

Whenever you lose your way,
Seek your truth within, not without.

It does not matter what others think.

It is your wholeness that must be explored.

Your yin and your yang
Must be expressed fully
For you to achieve realization
Of your true potential.

Your hurts are there as a mirror,
So that you may view the blockages
Within your own system.

There are no barriers to love.

Love transcends all.
Love protects and cloaks you.

You must never instil
Your weaknesses onto others,
And neither should you accept
Another's weakness, onto you.

*You must be clear as to what is truth,
And what is deception.*

Deception comes in many guises.

*Do not let your past fears
Cloud your mind into believing
That, which is not true.*

*You have love abounding from
Every corner of your universe.*

*Yet many of you will deliberately choose
To contemplate your navel,
And find fault in that
Which has no fault.*

*We say, start afresh with new goals,
And with new insights
That will support
And nurture you.*

Destructiveness has no purpose.

*It will cloud your mind,
And trap you in the past.*

*Constrictions in your life
Are all of your own making.*

*See obstacles as pebbles you can use
To skip upon the surface,
Not to trip up on, or slip and fall,
With no chance of arising.*

*You must be open.
You must love unconditionally.
You must receive love freely
Without reservation or mistrust,
And honour those close to you,
With every part of your being.*

Be generous in spirit.

Be truthful and sharing.

*Give generously to others,
Every part that is
The real 'you'.*

*Know that you are always safe,
For you will be held close
And comforted as you grow
And reach out.*

Faith, Hope and Charity

Hunger is not an outcome
Of a world shortage of food.
It is the result of a world gone awry
In the principles of charity, hope and love.

It is indeed sad when the opulent
Feel the need to hang on for grim death,
To that which may leave them lacking
In the areas of immortal purity of their souls,
Bereft of the virtues that render their souls
Peaceful and in harmony.

Poverty and hunger
Are no more than symbols of a world in crisis;

A world where each lives, not in unity with each other,
Not in unity with the life force,
Not in unity with nature, and not in unity
With the universal laws of nature.

To live like this is to condemn yourself to a life
Bereft of peace and bereft of joy and love.

When love and charity fill your life,
Your spirit is full and this fullness overflows.

There is then no need to hold onto anything,
For it is the sharing that brings with it
The joys of abundance.

The feast is enjoyed more
When it is shared.
The harvest is cherished more
When the field is planted in unison
And tended by a loving heart, and limbs
Eager for the experience of fruitful labour.

All work should be seen as a labour of love,
And love should be injected into all work,
Even the most dextrous or laborious of tasks.

Without this, work becomes a chore
Leaving the soul heavy.

The soul yearns for peace
And lightness of being.

Be in the light.

*Surround yourself with light beings,
And with positive souls,
Committed to a life of harmony
And cohabitation.*

*A life that is lived in peace
Is a joy till the end,
And when the end comes,
It is seen as a new beginning
At the side of God. . . a joyous resurrection
Of the rightful place of the spirit.*

*Give of yourself.
Share your possessions
As well as the fruits of your labour.
Exalt yourself to the highest level of your being.*

*Become all that you can be.
Test your strength.
Be patient and kind,
And at all times,
Be open to the gifts of the universe
That will fill your need.*

*Do this in order that you may reach
Even greater heights and greater love.*

Finding Fulfilment

Why do people have a need to see Fortune Tellers?

People's lives are fraught
With emptiness and longings
That seem to them to be unfulfillable
Using the resources at hand.

This is why people turn to strangers.

Strangers have no preconceived ideas,
And they have no expectations.
A stranger will listen in a way
That a friend or close one can't.
A stranger often wants
To make a good impression,
So the conversation is usually a positive one
As neither party has a vested interest
In the outcome.

The connection is usually time limited
So the drain on the psyche is minimal.

*No one has the potential
Of being hurt in this encounter,
Yet it has the persona of a very deep
And meaningful contact.*

*All it is, is an outlet in a way
That gains you a sense of peace,
Acceptance, connection, understanding
And unconditional love.*

*You glimpse yourself from another's positive view,
Not realising that you can do this
For yourself at any given time,
But choose not to.*

*It seems more real
When it comes from without.
What is it that has happened to you,
Where self-doubt is so prevalent?
Where self-deception is considered
More appropriate than self-love?
How can you ever hope to fulfil
Your destiny, dreams and potential
When you can't appreciate
Your strengths and your majesty?*

You would rather put yourself down
And call it modesty,
Than to challenge your fears
And go forth with strength
And purpose in being
All that 'you' are.

The mighty in this world
Do not hold a special secret,
Nor do they have special powers.

You must find your own greatness
And exalt in that.

Greatness is nothing short of
'Wholeness of purpose'.

Trust in the divine,
In the truth that comes
With a life lived true and full.
Always do your very best.

Always strive.

Always be true and go forward.

Finding Life's Purpose

The flow of life is not easy to achieve
For you must dwell deep
In the soul of 'who' you are.

Your intentions must always be
To live true to your purpose.

But how do you find
Your life's purpose?

It is not in the finding,
It is in the being.
Be-in-'G' . . . Be in 'God'
For God is your wholeness.

The sheer simplicity
Makes you duplicitous,
For in your human form
You are not always
Loyal to yourself.

*You are taught from a very early age
To be mindful of others;
Their thoughts, deeds
And reactions.*

*This would not be injurious to you
If you were only taught
At the same time,
The responsibility of self,
And the maintenance
Of the wholeness
And the goodness within.*

*It is not for anyone
To be in judgement of another.*

*Judgement is injurious
To the growth of the spirit.*

*It alludes to a difference,
And of one being
Better than the other.*

*Differences are what make you unique,
And it is in this uniqueness that you find
Harmony with others.*

*It is this uniqueness that must blend
To give wholeness.*

*Take and receive joyously knowing
That to do so is to open yourself up
To greater blessings and greater abilities.*

*Your human existence must teach you about love,
Not romantic love, but love of self
And love of others.*

*Not all are easy to love,
And it is sad to see so many spirits
Damaged and afraid.*

Fear keeps spirits locked.

*Love with your uniqueness
And reach a soul today.
Plant a seed of goodness
In someone's heart.*

*You do not know what may grow.
Just know that 'you'
Can make a difference.*

Follow Your Dream

*The soul must receive nourishment
And this comes in many forms.*

*The body also accepts nourishment
And this comes from a clean lifestyle.*

*The heart is the driver,
The ruler, the motivator.*

*For that which you love
Is that which you pursue.*

*When you are out of step
With your true purpose,
You feel an emptiness
That finds no satisfaction.*

*Like a well that is dry,
That no one visits.
Like a brilliant sunset
Behind a cloudy sky.*

You must commit to your Life Purpose.

You must follow your dream.

*You must have faith that the path
Will be made clear.*

*You must have confidence
In all of your abilities.*

*You must stretch your view of yourself
To encompass the essence
Of your life force.*

*It is this, that will drive you
To peace and fulfilment.*

*Your ego is but a deterrent.
Your ego is as a mirror with bad lighting.*

*You must make the effort to bathe your words
In laughter and let the ripples
Extend outward.*

Fulfil Your Heart

*Go as you will in the
Direction of your dreams.*

*Allow your thoughts to be the vessel
Upon which you glide.*

Fulfil your heart and be at peace.

*Find your pivotal point.
For this is your starting point,
From which you choose left or right.*

*Find your momentum.
Allow us to push you forward.*

*You will see in your mind's eye,
Where it is you need to focus.*

Allow us to direct your thoughts.

*All that is needed is for you to connect to your heart,
For when you do what you love,
There is never any doubt.*

When you are living in fear,
Everything that you are thinking
Will become your reality.

You are most powerful when your
Heart and mind are connected,
And when your eyes can only see forward
In the direction and fulfilment
Of your life's passion.

When you question what it is that you need to do,
Think only on your need for the moment.

Your truth will surface
When you see in the heart of another.

And when you look in the mirror
And see your own heart,
(Not your breathing heart),
But your heart that is full of love.

You need to fulfil your dreams.

Allow us to help you.

Grief

When your heart is heavy;
When your tongue finds no voice;
When the answers are not forthcoming
And the questions arise continuously
Inside your mind in a sorrow
You hold so deep.

When the call to action is strong,
But your body is unable to respond as you wish it to.

When life is merely
An existence rather than a
A joyous experience.

Just know that this is all
A part in the human process
That is known as grieving.

And know that whilst it's process
Has its hold over you,
It is normal to feel real limitations
In all you do and in all you are.

In your mind you may understand
The reasons and the logic
Of that which has befallen you
Or your loved one.

You may have a very clear understanding
That the person's time was nigh,
That they have run their race,
And that the essence of them
Is better served in the afterlife,
Rather than with you,
Here on the earth plane.

Please, we ask of you, feel no guilt
In the passing of a loved one,
For that will leave your soul
With a burden you cannot shake off,
And one that slows your progress,
As well as your loved one
On their journey in the afterlife.

Journeys of the soul are very different
To journeys of the mind.

The clarity of the soul
Holds no malice, no blame,
And knows no time.

It just is, in all purity.

It is all knowing, and it is all truth.

It is encapsulated in the true essence
Of a love that is both
Pure and unconditional.

It is the true love of the self
And the true essence of the soul
Which you are called upon
To transpose within and without.

The body is your carriage
Through this lifetime.

When you leave this life it only means that
The burden is lightened.

Therefore, do not grieve the loss
Of the essence of the soul,
Because this will always stay
Within you and as a part of 'you'

It is your soul that drives your purpose,
Past, present and future.

Happiness

Honour yourself in
All that you think,
In all that you feel,
In all that you say,
And in all that you do.

Let the outer 'you' reflect a central core
Of being at peace within.

This is what happiness is about.

When you are at peace within,
You become resilient to that
Which sharpens your tongue.

You do not need to raise your defences
When your central fortress
Is strong and resilient.

You do not need your armour when you feel
No shame in your vulnerabilities.

You do not need to strike out at another
When you are content.

*It is fear that drives the anger.
It is fear that causes you pain.*

*Faith, hope and charity
Will always see you through.*

*When you realise this, you can rest easy,
No matter what befalls you.
You cannot be at peace
When you are at odds with yourself,
And this oddness shows in the imbalance
Of your emotions and behaviour.*

You must strive for congruency.

*You must set your roots in fertile soil
So that you may grow
Resilient, pliable and yielding.*

*You must give voice to your own thoughts
And to your own ideas.*

*Others may not agree
But this is not to be perceived
As a negative thing.*

It is through differences
That ideas develop and become shaped.
This is the growth factor of the human soul.

You cannot survive in isolation.

You need nourishment
For your mind and your soul.

And just as the body detests the influx of toxins,
The same is true of the mind and of the soul.
Negativity is the toxin of the mind.
If let go, it will run through you
Like weeds in a garden
And can make idealism superfluous.

You must constantly weed out
The negative thought patterns
Before they turn to seed.

They must be eradicated and eliminated
And the only way to do this
Is to set up barriers to their procreation.
It is easy to take the road to negativity,
To give in to gossip, sarcasm and criticism.

*All of these stem from a lack of self-worth,
A feeling of aloneness.*

*What you need to strive for,
Is a feeling of oneness, not only with others,
But also with yourself.*

*Accept the multitude of discrepancies
That make up 'you'.
Then bring all of 'you' together
In a way that brings joy to others.*

*Make peace with yourself by putting the pieces
Of the jigsaw of 'you' together
So that each piece fits your life
And reflects your ideals,
Making your world—inner and outer
A better place to live.*

*Peace exists in a heart that is full,
In a smile that is shared,
In laughter that tickles the very essence
Of your being, and unlocks
The chains that hold you stagnant
And opens your eyes to the beauty
And wonderment that is 'you'
And your world.*

Heart, Mind and Soul

What befalls you is nothing less
Than your perception of your reality.

You must amass
The complexity of a universe
That offers much to your intellect
And level of understanding,
And accept that the world
Is not always as it seems,
But is always as it is.

This concept is a paradox
To a mind that relies on rationality.

But it rings true to a mind
Open to the boundless complexities
Of a knowing and a trusting
That is greater than the mind,
But not as great as the soul.

The soul is the pivot upon which
All knowing spins.

*The mind is the detector of matter
And is what limits you in your knowing.*

*In order to live true,
You must be true to what you know.*

*In being true to what you know,
You must often ignore that
Which has been taught to you,
And instead look within
To what resonates loud and clear,
With the love and light that lies within.*

It is not for you to question 'who' you are.

*It is for you to be wholly 'what'
And 'who' you are.*

*You must be a seeker of the light,
And a seeker of the truth.*

*And you must reside
In a place within your soul
That is touched by the hand of God.*

Inspiration

Breathe in truth.
Breathe out wisdom.

Truth within, which is then
Expressed in wondrous deeds
Is what the fire of inspiration sets alight.

When you focus on
The narrative of your life,
You become bogged down
In the tiny details and forget the ripples
That change the tides of time and your life.

None of you are truly aware
Of the small pebbles
In your lives that have
Such far-reaching effects.
Is it a person?
Is it a place?
Is it a time?
Is it an experience?

It is all of these;
Yet it is none of these.
It is often when your soul
Is at its lowest ebb,
That you open your heart
To the universe to provide inspiration.

To inspire is to take in.
Often you are closed to
The entire rationale of this,
Becauser you pursue your own desires
Instead of fulfilling your true purpose.

When you are in tune,
You are then open to receive
And take in all that is there
For the taking.

When you take this into your heart
You learn to live fully.

Each step, each task, each thought
Is then based on truth,
Love and integrity.

*Life is a journey
And you meet many
On your path.*

*Some you see as obstacles,
Not realising their true worth
In the order of things.*

*In your estimation, your life
Would have been better
Without them,
And you try in earnest
To forget their memory.*

*I say remember,
And remember well
All that you have
Learned from them,
And all that you have become
Because of them.*

*Remember the ripple effect,
And remember also
The laws of cause
And effect.*

*You need irritations in your life
As well as upheavals,
In order for you to find your true self,
And in order that you may
Grow into yourself.*

*The pearl is formed in response to
An unforeseen irritant.*

*Whilst it is forming, it is encased in
A protective shell.*

*So too is your soul
Encased in your body.*

*See your world as your oyster,
And become the pearl within.*

*Know your true worth
As an individual,
And celebrate all that you are,
And all that you become
As a result of the world
You are in.*

It's Your Choice

As human beings,
You are given a wondrous gift.

You have the gift
Not only to give voice to your ideas,
But also the gift to express
Your thoughts, with emphasis
On the emotional component.

This way, you can
Show your true self,
For in giving voice and action
To all that you say,
You mark your intent
Upon the world.

The joyousness from your integrity
Is boasted upon the minority.

You may in all good conscience
Have just intentions,
But it is in the delivery of these
That many fall short.

*In order to be credulous,
Your body must believe your thoughts.*

*This is why you must look
To the language of the soul.*

*This is seen in your eyes
And also in your gestures,*

*Do not trust the man
Who cannot show his hand,
For there is a mistrust in himself first.
And one who cannot trust himself,
Cannot be trusted by another.*

*We often talk in analogies,
But the message
Is very blunt here.*

*Trust is integral to truth.
Truth is integral to life.*

*Love cannot survive
In an atmosphere
Bereft of these virtues.*

Therefore, in any encounter,
You must first look at the true measure
Of the person and see them first
As they see themselves.

There is often present the cloak of shame
Which brings forth the mistrust
Of one's abilities.

This is put on a person,
And the challenge of
The measure of the person,
Is how they wear this cloak.

Some wear it as a crown of glory.

They parade around in it in order to avoid
The responsibilities of becoming fully
What God intended - The full creation.

This is also an avoidance
Of life lived fully.

Others may show the cloak
As but another appendage
That has had its use,
And can be discarded
For brighter garbs.

You should never forget
The effect of environment
And the influence of those you love
Upon your fragile self.

This is how you grow.

The end result can be
A fragrant fertile harvest,
Or a barren field
Not fit to reap.

It is your choice.
But in saying this,
You must not feel angered
With those that put shame
And fear upon you.

You must instead give thanks
For the opportunity to bloom
Amongst the thorns,
As the rose blooms
When watered and pruned
And put in fertile soil.

The seed is set.

The patent is laid down.

The harvest is the result
Of free will and choices.

Make your choices wisely.

Let these show in a light heart,
In a willing smile
And a hand
Reached out
In gratitude.

Integrity

*Integrity in all you say
And in all that you do
Brings about the cleansing
Of your heart and opens you up
To the juice of life.*

*The ebb and flow
In human conviction wanes,
And must in turn not be blocked
By false intentions,
Or criticisms that do not come
From love.*

*To share your feelings
Is a noble feat,
In context with the propriety
Of the act.*

*Falsehood is the brother of evil,
For light cannot shine
Through lies and deceit.*

Joy

The joys in life are found in an open, loving heart
That seeks no fault and sees no blame,
But one that entrusts and gives freedom to the spirit.

The spirit must be able to be free,
In order that the body that it dwells within,
May fully complete the assignment
That was bestowed before birth.

Human intervention and another's will,
Are in conflict with the intentions laid out.
Goodness will always prevail,
When it is recognised and observed.

Truth and integrity are vital to true living.
For to live without these is just a life of farce,
And such a life cannot be tolerated by a pure soul.

Friends are balm to your soul.
Your voice must be heard to resonate with another.

Comfort is a necessity, not a luxury
Which is experienced in a mutual
Understanding and commitment.

Just Be You

*Misconception is the key
To your answers.*

A different slant is needed.

*Allow the truth to unfold to heal the rifts,
And to make sense of the uncomfortable,
Felt like a pebble in your shoe.*

*You've tread so long in other's shoes.
It's time for the refit
Into a bolder, brighter 'you'.*

*Ashes to ashes, dust to dust;
The flow of life goes on,
Like a river to the sea;
Like larva spilt on virgin soil,
Destroying all in its path
With heat and fumes.*

*Only to give rise
To growth and abundance,
Not realising that the earth
Will give all it has.*

Seeds grow when the time is right

*The plains become flooded
When the seasons dictate.*

*Fire consumes the innocent,
Leaving in its wake devastation
As well as hope for new life.*

Life contains a paradoxical message.

*You must see that out of all misfortune,
You will find the key to your truth,
And to your reality.*

Life becomes as you see it.

*Your reality is only your perception
Of the vast array of opportunities.*

Some you take.

Most lay dormant.

Opportunities arise in everyday adversity.

*The pot of gold stands there ready
At the beginning of the rainbow.*

*Spend it well in times of drought,
For it is only the rain that brings out
Your brightest lights to behold.*

*We guide you on your path,
In this - your solo journey;
One that is unknown to another
And one that must be trodden
True and firm - but always on your own.*

Plant each foot square and true on solid soil.

Allow momentum to take you through.

*Follow your instincts
And be guided by your truth.*

Integrity is the key.

Believe in yourself.

Be you.

Knowing Yourself

When you're lost inside,
The only thing you can do
Is to find your way back to you.

It starts in life with being told what to do.

You're always told 'NO'!
At the precise time that you feel
You want to go in a certain direction.

Often you are left with a feeling of confusion
That permeates your life.

Each time you make a decision in your own right,
A booming voice says 'NO'!

Interesting, that the English language
Writes 'NO' and 'KNOW' and does not differentiate.

Why not have 'KNOW' sound the same as 'YES'?
This is where the dilemma arises.

*Inside of you, each time
You feel you 'KNOW' something
It feels like 'NO'.*

*The Eastern world is less complicated.
They teach the child from an early age
To go within, and to trust
The instincts from within.*

*In Western cultures, things are learned from without.
Then, as an adult, you have to find
Your road back within.*

*You must then find different pathways in order
To find peace in your existence.*

So how is this done?

*The numerous texts do hold many keys,
But the secret is in the divine.*

*It is in the acceptance of the self.
It is in your feelings of worthiness.
It is your self-destructiveness
That leads you away from yourself.*

*Always choose in favour of the self;
Not in the self-destructiveness of you,
But in the pure dignity of your being.*

*The mere fact of your existence
Is a miracle to behold.
You must appreciate your goodness
And your own inherent fortune
And become 'who' you are.*

*Genetics plays Russian Roulette
And the dice fall as a seed on the ground
That produces its offspring.*

Not each seed sprouts.

*You must rely on the elements
Of earth, wind, water and air
And look to their combinations
In your earth form.*

*In your life, whenever you are lost,
Look at which element is missing in your life
And work towards achieving wholeness
Within yourself.*

*All too often you denigrate yourself
And this is why you feel undeserving.*

*You blame your teachers
When they were sent to you
To teach you the lesson
Of self-directed learning.*

*It is each individual's choice
To enact their own perception of reality.*

This is what you see when you look at others.

Each person lives out their own perceptions.

*Many perceptions mean delusions.
Many delusions in our world auger bad.*

*You must reconnect to the real truth
In yourself, in other people, and in the divine.*

*Believe in unconditional love
For there are no other meanings
For love.*

Learning To Love

*You hold the answers
To every question,
And you must find the keys
That will unlock
The wisdom within.*

*It comes to some as the voice of reason;
To others it comes as the voice of experience;
But to all it comes as life's passage
In the journey within.*

*Some of you will be nurtured
In this struggle to bloom.*

*Others will find themselves strapped
In the cycle of despair and failure.*

*It is only by looking within
And seeing yourself as the unique,
Wonderful creation that you are,
That you will come to accept the beauty of everything
And everyone around you.*

*Relationships are true mirrors
Of your self-worth and of your sense
Of 'who' you are.*

*When you accept someone
In your inner sanctum,
You will only do so
With someone whose vibration
Beats similar to your own.*

*When you are in a dark space,
You do not want to be blinded
By the brilliance of another.*

*You will choose to be with those
Who are non threatening,
And with those who are a mirror
Of what you see within yourself.*

*In theory, the ideal of love
Is something that you can accept.
However, a soul that believes that
It does not deserve love,
Is one that cannot accept love.*

It falls away as it sticks only to the surface,
For it will be unable penetrate,
Just like oil cannot penetrate water.

The barriers must first be broken down,
And this can only be done
By the thoughts that pervade
A tired and weary soul.

Thoughts that raise the vibration,
And thoughts of self-loathing,
Must be replaced initially with words
Of encouragement and acceptance,
Of the true identity that is
Afraid of being identified.

You will all harbour self-doubts at times.

It is only the degree and perseverance
Of these thoughts that defines
Your self-worth.

Self-worth is the price tag you put on yourself,
Not realising that you are each priceless.

*There is not one person
Who is an exact replica of another,
And just as an ancient artefact is invaluable,
Your uniqueness makes you
Irreplaceable in value.*

*When you look to build relationships with others,
You need to see the true value
In all that is unique to them,
All the while understanding
The human need for acceptance,
Recognition and ultimately love.*

*Love is that strange word
Used to describe the simplest of feelings,
And the most complex of interchanges.*

Love will challenge every thought you have.

Yet love can simplify your life considerably.

*If you live with love as your one and only signpost
Along the maze of indecisions and travails in your life,
You will indeed be remunerated and live
A true, full and abundant life.*

*None of you need to learn how to love.
You only need to see through the facades
That pose as love.*

*Love is the peace that comes
When you behold the beauty
In yourself, in others and in
The environment you live in.*

*Love is the happiness found in the realisation
That each moment you have
Is yours to appreciate.*

*Open the barriers and love will come to you,
In every encounter, and in every situation,
For love is free to all.*

*Love is that rare commodity that is never-ending.
The more you give,
The more you have to give.*

*Fill your being and let it overflow onto everyone,
Through a smile, a touch
Or through laughter.*

Learn To Fly

When you listen with your ears,
You will only hear sound.

When you engage your brain,
The sounds start to differentiate,
And you become aware
Of all the nuances you hear.

When your mind is still,
Rather than hearing
The choir of the birds,
You become aware of
Each individual sound.

You hear the laughter of the kookaburra.
You hear the sound of action in the wings.

You feel the breeze that creates
The bird's uplift.

You hear the drop of water
That gives sustenance and life.

In order to fly, you must hear the call.

*You must find the currents
Upon which to glide.*

You must have mastery over yourself.

*You must learn and master
How to get up to the heights
You wish to reach.*

*Then each and every evening,
As night shadows fall and darkness ascends,
You must find your resting place.*

*You must find that place,
High and sheltered where you once felt safe.*

*That place of tranquillity,
Away from predators.*

*That special place away from
All that may be of harm to you,
And just rest easy.*

Let Go and Let God

The heart beats rhythmically.

*The mind thinks in logic and is linear.
It chooses thoughts and direction.*

The eyes see beauty or lacklustre.

The ears hear words of calm or tempest.

And it is the voice that speaks of truth or lies.

*When all your senses are in unison,
You will pass through your life
As a locomotive on a straight track.*

*The obstacles in your life are only hiccoughs,
So do not be distracted by them.*

*You must always play out your life
To its fullest and not limit yourself
To your plans alone.*

God overseas all.
He has a master plan
Which encompasses everything
That you must endure, enjoy and experience
In order for your heart to sing,
And your soul to dance.

You must aim for the highest level
You can reach on this soul plane.

Your life might sometimes seem to lack direction.

When this happens, look within
To that place of peace and love.

You must stop externalising, procrastinating,
Dramatizing and catastrophizing.

You have a life given to you as a gift.

Enjoy each moment.
Rejoice in every travail.
Conquer your fears.
Relish your achievements.
Proclaim your greatness.
Share your riches.

*And always remember that love and peace
Are your greatest strengths.*

*Everything you do in their names
Will bring you to a higher place
Within and without.*

*To fulfil yourself within,
You will never be without.*

*To fulfil yourself from without,
You will only tap into your neediness,
And your sense of nothingness.*

*Exalt yourself to your rightful place,
And learn to accept the richness
Of all life has to offer you.*

*Grab at it with both hands,
And appreciate your place in
The order of things.*

*Life is your gift to yourself.
Your gifts, used with love,
Are your gifts to life.*

Love

You must trust that the Universe
Will give you all that you need,
So be patient and trusting
And it will come to pass.

You are all children of God
And He will not let you down,
For the flowers of Heaven must be watered.

Life's teardrops are but splashes
On the whirlpool of life.

God will give freely
When you open up your heart
And your soul to Him.

He will not see you hungry
For laughter or for love.
He will nourish your being
And cleanse your heart,
In order that you may be free
To love and to serve.

*Pain in your heart
Is merely a denial of your soul*

*Your best output is derived from your wholeness
And want to be nought but what you are.*

It is enough!

*Never forget that you are all
God's little flowers and
Now is your time to blossom
And show your real colours
And splendour for all to partake
And receive nourishment from.*

*God loves his wildflowers,
As He does all his perfect ornamentals.*

*He fills the stem
That holds the flower upright,
And gives it the sap
Which he breathes into it – into 'you'.*

*You are loved completely
If you just open your heart and feel it.*

Making Your Life Count

You are stuck in your own life
And you take this as a test of yourself.

You see yourself as a failure not realising
There is no such thing as 'failure'.

'Failure' is a word
That means little more
Than to give up on yourself.

To go forward
Is often the easiest option,

And yet it is something
That very few people do
When they are at a so-called
Standstill in their lives.

There is no such thing as standing still
For the Universe continues.

Each breath you take, brings about a mixture
Of chemical reactions.

For most of you, this is
The simplest metaphor to explain
That each action has an equal
And an opposite reaction.

Each breathe that you
Involuntarily breathe in,
Leads to the breathe out,
In order that the next gulp of air
Can be inhaled.

You should look upon your life
As you do each breath you take.

Inhale everything that is good for you.

Do this automatically.
Then decipher everything
That is not necessary to sustain you
And make you grow.

Look forward to this unending cycle.

This is what life is—an unending cycle
Of life-giving sustenance;
An ebb and flow;
Action and reaction.

You complicate your life
By your emphasis placement.

You need to know what it is,
That you need for your growth.

You need to accept love in all its forms,
And reject the fear that keeps you stagnant.

The plan for your life
Is already determined.

Free will is the choice you have
To either accept and nurture your gifts,
Or to reject yourself and your gifts,
And thereby make a life for yourself
That is steeped in sorrow,
Pain and misery.

When you feel the pain of rejection,
You must remind yourself that this stems
Wholly from within yourself.

You accept rejection as a slight upon yourself,
And believe that you are unworthy of another.

Instead, you must accept
Another's choice as simply that;
A decision based on a personal opinion,
One that negates the opinion you have of yourself.

You must free your mind
Of negativity and pessimism;
A doom-and-gloom outlook.
Instead, fill your mind with the awe of a child,
In wonderment of the miracle that is 'you'.

You are wholly and solely a being of light,
And you must illuminate yourself
In order to fill the earth
With light and love.

This will dispel the fear and angst
That is rife in your community.

*Each mistake is but another tread
On the step to enlightenment.*

*Be grateful for each obstacle,
For it provides another opportunity
To grow and define the
True being of who 'you' are.*

Give in to the passion of life.

Live life fully.

Open your eyes and see the beauty.

Open your heart and feel the love.

Open your mind and know the peace.

*Then walk as you must
To the goal of your life,
Living wholly and fully in total knowing
Of the wonderful person you are
And continue to become.*

Marriage

Marriage between two people,
Is the true journey of hearts,
Of minds and of souls,
For in this union comes
The true expression of oneness.

To be at one with another,
You must first be at one with yourself.

When the heart speaks,
You must listen;
Not to the whims of fancy fare,
But to your inner longing
For completeness.

A relationship that is pure,
Shares the same dynamic as the sea.

It ebbs and flows and just as each wave
Is different, so too is each encounter.

In marriage, as in every relationship,
You must always find joy
In the essence of another's being.

You do this through touch,
But mostly you do this through thought.

Your thoughts govern what is to come.

At times you may find yourself
In denial of your part in the destructiveness
Of some of the negativity that you manifest,
But the decision and free will of every action,
Lies embedded in your choices
As well as in your actions.

To avoid bad decisions, you must look
To the clouds - feather-soft and protective.

Know also that they have the capacity
To emit great shards of lightening in an instant.

This is how your words can strike!

Look at your relationships as a cloud,
Soft and sometimes overshadowing.

As you rest on your laurels,
So too will the grains of sand
Cease to flow through the portals
Of your relationship.

Emptiness and shadows will then replace
The true joyous radiance of spirits
Joined as God intended.

In relationships, there is no room
For the destructiveness of a tongue
That speaks not from the heart.

Each step you take must be in harmony.
And, although on the same path,
You must accept diversions and greener pastures
Along the way.

The heart needs tossing in order to sing.

You must lift yourself to new heights,
And give yourself over to the wonderment
Of the true essence of another.

Allow yourself to be touched purely,
Reverently, and with no thoughts
Of gain or possession.

Love comes free.

It is a gift that you give.
It is a gift that, as you give it,
You also receive it.

It does not exist as love,
If this interchange does not happen.

It is the one thing that exists in duality,
And in opposing forces uniting.

As the lightning strikes
Upon the unseeing ground,
So too does your unsuspecting form,
Feel catapulted by the feelings
That love induces.

It is a force greater than any that exists,
Yet many do not honour or respect it
For the profound benefits
That it can create within them.

Meditation

By meditating, you are in control
Of the perception you have of
The workings of your mind.

This is not in fact the case,
Because when you meditate,
You give yourself over to the will of another.

True meditation is not a process
Of following orders.

It is being pure;
Pure of thought,
Pure of heart,
And open to receive
With no expectation
And no human desire.

There is much that is gained
On a materialistic level
By those who portray themselves
As gurus others must look up to.

It is indeed a fact that some people
May need direction and guidance.
And it is indeed a blessing to be shown a light,
When darkness prevails.
But this is not to be rewarded
In material ways.

For you to reach your journey within,
You must always be aware of others around you,
And wherever possible, shine your light
For others to see and to follow.

There is no right or wrong
In your journey within.

The evil comes into play,
When this is a journey of the head
And not one of the heart.

Not all people are at peace
With themselves or within themselves.

Most do not relish the silence,
And try in earnest to fill the void
And fill it quickly with clatter and clutter.

No wonder you become lost.

You must learn to use each of your senses.
Challenging yourself to do so fully
And to appreciate each in turn.

To see true beauty, is to see
With your heart and soul.

Your eyes merely draw you to all that
You should be bringing into your being.

Once again 'We' speak of being,
And if you were to segregate and confine
The real meaning of meditation,
It is 'pure being'.

'Be in God'

You will then feel a completeness and contentment
Within yourself that allows your mind to rest
And to fully accept love.

Honour your being.

Breathe in the God force,
And breathe out the wisdom
That lies within.

Be kind to yourself and allow yourself
To go in the direction your soul yearns for.

You will understand the path you have to follow,
When you can soften your intent
And go with the breath of the wind,
The tides of time
And the flow of the currents.

Nothing will befall you
Of a negative nature
When your heart is full,
And when your intention is
Clarity, Truthfulness and Godliness.

Love is your way to peace,
And peace is your way to love.

The two may be separate,
But one cannot come
Without the other.

Old Age

*Age is a time-line that measures
Your presence on the earth plane,
In a way that is clear to your mind.*

*Your death is the bridge
That transgresses your mortality
And helps you to enter into the realm of the divine.*

*The soul has no concept of linear time.
It can only understand the mere format
Of life essence in its true form.*

*In death you stand at the precipice
Of time immortal.*

It is a difficult concept to grasp.

*As such,' We' tell you in terms
That matches your understanding,
Limited though this may be.*

In age you will glimpse your mortality.

In death you meet up with your immortality.
You then go forth in a form that is the
True essence of all that you are.

This is why it is of paramount importance
To honour all that 'you' are,
And to live your life authentically and true.

In doing this, your transition
To the afterlife will be a seamless one.

As you grow older, it may appear that
You grow weaker - this is only in your body.
Your soul remains timeless and this is
The essence of what carries you through
The debilitating factors of old age.

You should embrace these tests upon your spirit,
And know with certainty that you must give up
Your dependency on the worldly values
That you hold so dear.

You will then find your place on the earth
That is your niche.

Reaching Your True Potential

True inspiration is that vital ingredient
That is mixed in the gut of longing
And comes to fruition in the art of 'beingness'.

It is in your wholeness
And wish to be completely authentic,
That you can articulate your true being,
And thus become an inspiration
To yourself and to others.

It is incorrect to assume
That you can be inspired by others.

It is your perception of their actions,
Deeds, words and demeanour
That resonates with that part within you,
That looks for completion and expression.

You are thereby drawn to that
Which lies as a vacuum within yourself.

This is the law of attraction.

*This is what gravitates you to others,
And others to you.*

*The heart must be still, so that the ripples
May reach it clearly and the feelings be felt
And accepted unconditionally.*

*It is therefore of great importance
What you perceive as lacking in your life,
Because you will fill your life with that
Which becomes your focus.*

*When you are most in need, do not contemplate
The misery of your situation.
Instead, place the emptiness
At the gates of opportunity, so that the void
May be filled in such a way as to bring
Contentment and completion towards you.*

*Do not ask for the impossible,
But expect that all will be provided
For your own wellbeing, and integrity.
The soul must be whole in order to fulfil
Its true purpose.*

*A sorry heart, A blocked mind,
An aching, weary body, and diminished perspective,
All lie in the face of, and as deterrents
And blockages to your completion.*

*To be inspired, is to recognise the need
Of the soul to reach new heights.
To soar as the eagle,
To laugh as the kookaburra,
And to sing as the thorn bird.*

*To offer yourself completely to what is required of you,
With no concern as to the outcome,
And to trust fully in the process
Of what is, and what is to be.*

*In being inspired,
You then become your own inspiration,
For the sparks ignited within bring about
An inferno of longing and striving
To be all that you are.*

*In feel complete, you must immerse yourself
In the here and now,
And want for nothing except to be secure
In your own cocoon of acceptance.*

Reality

What befalls you is nothing less
Than your perception of your reality.

You must amass the complexity
Of a universe that offers much
To your intellect and
To your level of understanding
And accept that the world
Is not always as it seems,
But is always as it is.

This concept is a paradox to a mind
That relies on rationality.

But this concept rings true
To a mind that is open
To the boundless complexities
Of a knowing and a trusting
That is greater than the mind,
Yet not as great as the soul.

The soul is the pivot
Upon which all knowing spins.

*The mind is the detector of matter
And what limits you in your knowing.*

*In order to live true,
You must be true to what you know.
In being true to what you know,
You must often ignore
That which has been taught to you.*

*Instead, you must look within
To what resonates loud and clear,
With the love and light that lies within.*

*It is not for you
To question 'who' you are.*

*It is for you to be
Wholly 'what' and 'who' you are.*

*You must become a seeker of the light,
And a seeker of the truth.*

*You must reside in a place
Within your soul that is touched by
The hand of God.*

Relationships

God in his wisdom knows what's best.
The left hand does not always have to know
What the right hand is doing.

When two hand are locked in love,
There is no room for doubt
Or misconstrued affection.

Love is a gift that belongs to everyone.

God's love is the glove
That snugly fits the hands of love.
Real love does not doubt.
Real love does not fear.

Be silent and listen to your heart.
It will tell you if it is real and if it is true.

The petals of the flower do fall,
But their joy is complete,
For they have bloomed
And lived to capacity.

*Where one flower falls
Another gives rise.
There is a time, and a season
For all things.*

*The shell of the past must be shed
So that a new beginning
Can come about.*

*Be fresh.
Be clean.
Be love.
That is all there is.*

*You must pray and believe
That all will come to you
As you need it.*

*Do not fret,
For there is one
Who will always protect.*

*When you feel hurt
Be sure that your focus
Is on what should be
And not what is.*

Do not lose sight of love.
And do not mistake what you perceive,
As your reality.

The giver will give to you,
That which you most desire,
And your happiness will be complete.

Do not ever withhold your love.
It is like holding back the tide.
It is not to be.

Give your love, and give it completely
To all around for that is your job.

Do not concern yourself
With others.

Live your own truths,
And always be true to yourself.

You cannot define another's life path,
No matter who it is.

Your life is of your own making.

*You must do everything to ensure
That your touching of another
Is in love and kindness,
Not in judgement.*

This is your way to peace.

*You must be gracious with your tongue.
And keep in check your misgivings.*

Do not worry.

Be kind in word.

Do not judge so harshly.

Lighten up.

*There is one who oversees all,
And knows all.*

*Look deeper within,
And you will know
The certainty you seek.*

Relationships 101

*Love is at the heart of all relationships,
And this must be your focus always.
This is what you must try to reach
As you go through the pitfalls of your lives together.*

*When love becomes elusive to you,
You must look to your focus placement.
Is your perception of the truth
Of greater importance, than the love
That is at the crux of your union?*

*When you distrust the hand
Offered to you in love,
It is only because of your fear
Of the intentions behind it.
You base this on your past negative
Perceptions and experiences.*

*Look for reassurances in love,
Even when none are offered
When and how you believe and think
That they should be offered to you.*

*Choose the path of least resistance
Do not argue a point,
Because that is all it is,
And you will lose.*

*You will find yourself stuck,
For you will be unable to go
In the direction that you wish to go,
Because of impediments that you
Have thrown in your own way,
That make you feel defeated.*

*'We' say to you to look for
The victory in the achievements
That you make each and every moment.*

*Your self worth is of great value,
And it is not something to be measured.*

*It is something you are,
And that is all there is to it*

*Realise that your goals
May not always be the same.*

The struggle comes from one with blinkers on,
And the other with fear,
Blocking the true path to light.
Have faith in your ability
And walk surefooted.

When steps are placed in your way,
Know that they have been placed there,
In order that you may learn
To climb to new heights.
They are not there for you
To trip up and stumble on.

Your pain will feel very real.
It is your test, to once and for all,
Not accept the view of another,
But to create your own reality,
And your own peace and tranquillity.

Give reassurances to others but
Be firm in your resolve for harmony within your soul.
Understand your reactions and learn
To move forward and not be stagnant.

Create ripples that radiate out
From a loving heart.

Do not fear consequences.
Instead, embrace new horizons.

When you are on the threshold
Of a new and distinct phase in your life,
You will need to break free the chains
That have held you back for so long.

You can only feel self-respect,
When you understand
And live your truth.

Any anxieties you feel are only
A torment of your old beliefs,
In contrast with what
You now know to be true.

Stand your ground
As to your congruency.

Allow yourself the luxury
Of what you need and enjoy.
Love is not your duty,
And neither is it your due.

It just is.

*There is no need to justify
What is done for love.*

*If it is not seen
For its simplicity and essence,
Then it cannot be seen.*

*Others have their own delusions,
And see what is in their heart
Mirrored back to them.*

*Do not strike back.
Instead, allow spaces.*

Love.

*Do not confuse love
For expectations met.*

Have faith in what is real.

*We will not leave you dry,
For the well of love is always accessible,
To those who know the value of all it holds.*

Rise Above Yourself

Your voice is such a tiny whisper.
And what you need to say,
Must not be said in haste
Or with vindication.

It should instead be stated
With clarity and purpose.

But what is your purpose?

Let your expectations
Become visibly clear to you,
And do not allow
The embers of past hurts mar the clarity
Of that which you know needs expression.

You speak of new beginnings!

But why should you seek a beginning,
When your beginning has long ago begun?

You have already breathed
Your first breath,
So therefore it can never
Be done again.

Instead of searching
For untarnished feelings,
Go beyond this to the exploration
Of the feelings in the here and now.

Then seek only what is relevant
In this moment,
And from this moment.

It is not as hard
As you may think.

In fact it is much easier to let go of that
Which is in the past and is irrelevant.

See purpose ... See truth
Seek out positive features
And tranquil thoughts.

Do not enchain your thoughts.

Do not impose your wants
And greed upon another.

Let thoughts be free.

Reality and truth
Will surface.

Do not invent problems.

Do not manufacture dramas.

Note the intent,
And if the intent is good,
Then whatever follows,
Must also be good.

Make new treads
On the stairs,
But only in order to
Reach new heights.

Romance

Love is that magical ingredient
That makes your life worthwhile.

It allows you to see through all the fog,
And gain clarity both into your own soul,
And also the soul of another.

There is comfort in the realisation
That you are no longer
On your own.
And that from here on,
You can rely on another
As a guide, a teacher,
A lover and a friend.

In a romantic relationship
It is important not to romanticise too much.

In this day and age romance has taken a shift
Into a new direction
That does not sustain love.

*Romance is the adventure
Of the soul to a place far away
From thoughts of yourself,
And towards thoughts of another.*

*Romance is doing something
Solely for the sake of giving
Long-term pleasure to another;
Not in the sense of buying
The person's affection or admiration,
But in the acknowledgment
Of doing something for another,
With no sense of self-gain.*

*This is what 'romance' is:
Two people committed to the needs
And pleasures of another,
And forsaking ego and reward
In the process.*

*As human beings you have
Many opportunities for love.*

*You must all see everyone
You come into contact with as special.*

*When love and relationship meet
As two people joined as one,
It comes as a very special gift;
One you must accept fully and respect.*

*To be in love, is to experience
An upliftment of the soul;
A new chance at life;
And a chance to create new life,
Within the comfort and security
Of a loving union.*

*When a love such as this enters into your life,
You should not question it.*

*You should not stand in judgement,
Nor should you accept the judgement of others.*

*To find your soul mate you must first search
Within your own soul and be a true expression,
Inner and outer of 'who' you are.*

*Then and only then will you recognise another
And see into their true being.*

Self Esteem

Self-esteem is not only a matter
Of what you think of yourself,
It comes as a gift when you are
At one with God and all creation.

You must see yourself always,
As a very vital part of the whole.
Enjoy your goodness and your gifts.
They are given to you in order
That you may relate in a way that far belies
Your expectations of yourself.

There is always room
For the majestic to arise in you,
So you may reach higher peaks
And fly as you should.

When in doubt, look no further
Than the abundance that 'you' are,
For it is impossible to doubt yourself,
When you reach deep in your soul
To the depths of your being

Self-Love

Violence has no place in relationships,
For it encompasses the will
Of one onto another and transgresses
The essence of pure love.

This is not to say that
The understanding of one's limits,
And control of one's emotion
Is not a factor at play.

It is that the control of one's emotive state
Must not be compromised in such a manner.

There is no room in a loving relationship
For actions that harm another.

You must take time to learn this concept.
And in learning this, you will also learn
About loving yourself.

It is not until you learn to fully love yourself,
That you will be able to love another fully.

This is a paradox and a paradigm.
For love is free to all.

It is something you give.
It is something you are,
Not something you demand.

If you have to ask of it or for it,
It is not there for you in its pure form.
This is not to say it does not exist.

When you experience it as lacking,
It is more likely that it is you
Who is lacking in faith or in truth.
You must reconcile within yourself,
That which is lacking in yourself
And not demand it from another.

Love, in order to grow, must be given freely.
You cannot demand terms.

Love does not understand duty,
Nor does it respect weakness.

Love is free and strong
And exists of itself.

Self-Worth

You are first and foremost human beings.

In your lives, you seem to segregate yourselves
And form partnerships to enhance
Your place in life.

Some people find themselves
Trapped in an identity
That is not of their making,
But one that society proclaims them to be.

These are the roles you believe
That you are expected to play.

When you see a man living a life
Not true to his calling,
You see an unhappy man.
A man lost with no clear view of the horizon;
A man who sees his reflection
In the shine of his shoes,
Not in the reflection of the stars.

*You sleep at night so that you may
Rest as the sun ebbs.*

*You should let your dreams stem
From a fulfilled heart,
A still mind and a nourished body.*

In peaceful slumber you find rest.

*In times of wakefulness,
You need to direct your full attention
On the personal journey that is your life.*

*Each path is individual.
Each encounter you have
Is an opportunity to find grace.*

*Each disagreement with another,
Is an opportunity for your growth.
Each opportunity for growth,
Gives you alternatives and choices,
Choosing to be righteous or to evolve.*

*Turn the other cheek does not mean
That you allow disrespect to befall you.*

It means: see another reality,
See another direction,
See another point of view,
See another perspective.

Who knows where this input may lead you.

Allow your eyes to see alternative paths.
For your way in life must include
Many alternate routes.
At the beginning of the day,
Press in your co-ordinates
And plan your trek.

Illuminate your mind and open your heart.

Be warm and steadfast.
Be kind and gracious.
Be discerning and loyal.
Be well tempered and restrained.
Be cautious and trusting.
Be loving and dignified.

If you are all of these things
You will shine and your light will fill
The darkness in others.

Your step will be the beacon
For others to follow.

Your voice will be the voice of reason
For discouraged, disgruntled, dejected,
And confused souls.

Your kindness will open doors
To opportunities for homeless souls,
Searching for a safe haven.

Command respect.
Give acceptance and encouragement.

You are all unique yet all the same.

It is your differences that highlight your strengths
As well as your weaknesses.

You should see each other as links
In the chains of life.

Each link is a circle complete
And never-ending.

*Interconnected, you can create
An abundance of circles
To form the true circle of life.*

Where one life ends another begins.

*When you are interconnected,
You achieve a much richer journey,
For you will no longer
Live in isolation and fear.*

*Instead, you will live your life
In harmony, abundance and in joy.*

*Each person has the ability
To join forces with another life partner,
And in doing this, they will
Increase their joy ten-fold.*

*Marriage is not a necessity of the soul,
But it is a necessity of the laws of society.*

*Marriage provides the basis
For the security and safety
That is lacking in your world today.*

Success In Life

Success in life
Is the ultimate reward
For a life lived true and full.

The human form seeks recognition
For deeds done well
In the form of trophies, money
And material possessions.

These are but outward shows
And have little meaning
When there is no intrinsic factor.

To feel success is to have
A true feeling of inner joy
At a job done well.

True success comes at the sharing
And the partaking of the feast,
Filling the bellies of the hungry.
Knowing that sustenance is achieved
Is what success is all about.

The Journey Of Life

Death is not in itself a difficult concept.
It is the transition of the life force,
That is difficult to comprehend.

You must adjust your perceptions
Of time and space
To conceptualise the alter ego
Of consciousness.

It is vague in its interpretation,
Yet the preciseness of death
Is unimaginable to
Your human perception.

You cannot liken it to anything you know
Therefore it cannot be.

When you are in your human form
You are human beings.

In your alternate state you become as one
With the God force that exists in all of you.

You then become something
That is of insurmountable explanation.
A speck in the universe,
A drop in the ocean.

Yet you are all at one
With the eternal magnitude
Of time, space and distance.

Your immortality is not to be questioned
And it is not to be compared with others.

Each of you has a role to fulfil.

Some are but muses
For the greatness of others,
But even in that role,
You have great significance.

Do not ever forget the significance
Of the smallest act of kindness.

It is these, in conglomeration,
That help change the world
And bring light into darkness.

You wonder as to the dark hours,
The suffering, the emotional disruption
And sorrow in its bitter sweetness.

These are not tests of strength or endurance.

These are merely your options
When your soul has lost its anchor.

For each person,
Life will throw you lifelines
In the form of people and experiences.

Some of you let go your ropes.
Some of you, entangle yourselves
In the ropes.
And others share their lifelines.

To anchor yourself through this
May appear safe,
But by doing this, you will not
Find the currents upon which to glide
When times or the winds
Are unfavourable.

You often do not forecast your journeys,
Nor make room for encounters
Or fair or unfavourable winds.

Passages of time become your enemy,
And you look to time
As something used against you;
As a force to be reckoned with,
Instead of a linear projection
Of all that is.

Your beingness becomes a burden
To yourself and to others,
And you lose authenticity
Of your true-self.

Your words become hollow and empty,
And your yearnings are for a connectedness
Within yourself and for an affinity
With the essence of others,
In like form.

The tempest is but a reminder
Of elements in harmony,
Producing a force
To be reckoned with.

Your journey in your beingness
Is to arrive at a safe place
Within yourself.

When you are born,
You know this principal.

Then you give over
To your parents all responsibility
For your sustenance
And for your existence.

At your death,
You again give up your control
And exist in the true faith
Of a oneness, even though
You no longer exist.

The Meaning Of Life

Life though difficult at times
Is a gift for you to enjoy.
It is the essence of your being
That reignites you many times over.

You must unite with others
So that you may see your light and shade.
Let your clarity of thought become evident.

You are all searching
For the meaning of life.

This is a ludicrous concept.
It is only by living out your life,
That you find true purpose.

Your only ultimate state of being,
Is at being at one with yourself;
In relationship with nature,
The elements and each other.

Tranquillity comes when you are
At peace with yourself.

*You find peace not through doing,
But through being your true self.*

You must not confuse the two.

*When it plays itself out, the two
Become one and are inseparable.*

*This is the true test of your
Accomplishment as human beings.*

*It is while you are separated
In this purpose that you question,
Not only yourselves,
But mankind as well
And find blame within the situation.*

It does not matter what you do.

*It is your performance of that task
That yields your productiveness.*

*You must endure much
In order to contemplate perfection.*

Balance is important in order
That you not upset your place
In the hierarchy of life.

Hierarchy is the pivotal point
Where each contributor in the planet
Sits at the point where they belong
And pivots from this point t
To create both change
And consistency at the one time.

Each being must have flexibility
To move freely from this point.

You cannot do this successfully
If you do not realise the point
Where you belong.

Recognise that special place
Where you rest and are at ease.

Why is it that you humans
Must always be different to what
And who you are?

*Is it your perceptions
Of what is good and evil,
What is acceptable, and what is not,
That makes you transgress
Who 'you' are?*

*You are each given many opportunities
To exert your true selves,
Just like the drop of water does
In a ripple outward effect.*

*Water is clear and clean,
And doesn't ask anything of itself
Other than to flow, drop by drop
From the sky.*

*Each drop, though of no consequence in itself
Gives life to flora and fauna alike.*

*If only you could see yourselves
As drops of water.
If only you could realise your potential
To bring sustenance and new life,
And life abundant wherever you be,
And wherever you fall.*

Your concept of falling
Is again not a positive one.
You stumble, you graze knees, you get hurt.

You are not aware of just being.

You become exhausted with effort
And you do not realise that this is resistance
That is happening.

You make your thoughts rational
And give voice to opinion rather than truth.

Truth is blurred.

Opinion is only that—opinion.

When banded together it gives strength to
The human voice but not to the human heart.

Strength of purpose comes,
Not when there is no opinion,
But when there is only crystal-clear truth,
The kind that often belies explanation,
Yet in itself is indisputable because
It is the essence of what is.

Though complicated, one's life is
As simple as 'ABC' '1,2,3'.

The eagle does not stand on ceremony
Each time he stalks
And captures his prey.

He knows in order to be,
He must be 'who' he is
Despite what others may think of his action.

Killing for food as he does,
Is not against the laws of nature,
But is in keeping with them, and in keeping
With the balance spoken of earlier.

It is what man makes of this,
And the way that man
Identifies himself with the eagle
To justify his own killing spree.

It is not only the gunman who kills.
It is everyone who partakes
Without the need
That transgresses this law.

You are not eagles, so cannot be eagles.
You are neither inferior nor are you superior.
All that is possible, is for you
To achieve your rightful place.

The times ahead must be simplified
Because there are too many lost souls
Searching relentlessly in the dark.

You must help them see only their truth
And find their peace in their goal.
Reaching your goal is not
An achievement in itself.

Achievement comes with integrity.

Achievement is knowing
Who 'you' are,
Where 'you' are,
And what 'you' do,
So that there are no grey areas,
Only symmetry and balance.

Guin comes as peace
Not as power or money.

The Train of Life

You are first and foremost
A reflection of all that is within you.

It is the lightness or darkness of others,
That gives you the perspective
On yourself.

Do not worry about those
Who are only in your life
As 'observers'.

Your life has its own design,
And you are the driver on the tracks
We lay before you.

The train does not always go full speed,
And there is no turning back on the train of life.

You must accept many on your life's journey,
In order for you to be full of all that you need
To take you to that place of fulfilment
That is within you.

It is not for you to judge
Who must come on this journey.

You need to find balance
In order to stay well balanced yourself.

You will then see all of the alternatives
And choices available to you.

All that happens when you feel stuck,
Is a stopping point for you to reflect
And then continue on your journey,
Polished and ready for all there is
Waiting for you.

Rejoice in your choices to date,
For it is these that brought you
To this place where you need to be.

It is now time to bathe in these qualities of yours,
The biggest of these being those
That still lay dormant within 'you'.

Realize that your gifts are your gifts alone.
Realize that a gift is never a gift
Until it is given to another
Or shared in unison.

*Be brave, for you have yet to meet
Your true challenge and destiny.*

*Feel the ripples of excitement
As you come into yourself and learn
The true depths of your soul.*

*Realize that what often transpires in others,
Is the reflection in the mirror of that
Which you are trying to slough off.*

*Know also that this will stay on your psyche
Till you release it.*

*All that is needed now,
Is to release all that is superfluous,
And to release all that is no longer needed
And weighs you down.*

*Go forward,
Sure in the knowledge
That you are loved,
And you are protected,
And you are exactly that
YOU*

Thoughts

*Once upon a time,
A tiny speck existed
And from this, all matter
And all material things
As we know it, were created.*

*This is how a thought becomes an idea,
A principal, and a mantra.*

*This is why you must harness
And enjoy, create, and recreate
The tiny concepts, images and ideas
That frequent upon the flat screens of your minds.*

*It is not for you to determine
The importance of each thought,
For many appear to come 'Out of the blue'.*

*It is for you to grasp these random thoughts,
And pin them down with words
That will give them meaning.*

They come to you to ponder upon
And to challenge yourself
As to their validity
And their full meaning.

You must harness your thoughts
And give them form
By building them into sentences.

A thought, as of itself, rarely comes
With its own sentence.

It is your brain that structures it
And gives it so called clarity.

The clarity you give it are only your thoughts
Mixed with your vision for its inception,
Put upon the canvas of your beliefs
And experiences.

You then translate this through
Your limited knowledge and your vocabulary,
Into a filtered version of what came to you,
As but one star in the Universe.

This is why you must give homage
To some of your thoughts.

The astronomer seeks to find
The purpose for each star in the Universe.

You must do the exactly the same
With all the prominent and consistent
Thoughts that come to you.

These thoughts are there
To teach you about yourself,
And about your relationships,
Not only with yourself,
But with others as well.

That is the reality of what
The Universe symbolizes.

Do you stand out and shine
And declare your existence?
Or are you just a speck
That goes unrecognized?

No matter which you are,
Know that you are indeed
A part of the almighty plan.

*Your existence is neither
An accident nor an error in judgment.*

*What may appear as errant thoughts,
Are also not random.*

*They are specks and stars upon the canvas
That become the tapestry of 'you'.*

*Like a tapestry, the needle goes in
And comes out some.*

This is the pain of new ideas.

*To add colour and dimension,
You need always to dig into,
And through the layers of your outer being.*

Let it rest long and deep inside your soul.

*Then and only then can the needle emerge
To take up more thread and texture,
And become colour, light and shade,
And emerge as a multidimensional,
Or bland creation that others
Can connect to.*

*You might at times believe
That you are 'a victim of your fate',
You might also believe that
'Your fate befalls you'.
You may also say that
'You fall upon hard times.'*

*In saying and believing these things,
You do not give credence to the way
That you are in charge of developing
Your own destiny.*

*It is 'You' who chooses each thought
To be either a fleeting one,
Or one that you harness
As a concept or belief that you
Develop into your Mantra.*

It is 'You' who chooses the path that you take.

*It is 'You' who decides the 'when', the 'where'
And the 'how'.*

*Thoughts are the energy
Through which you develop your form.*

Your thoughts determine and guide
What you mould yourself into.

This is the reason that you
Must be discerning in your thoughts.

They will stick to you like 'stick-it' notes,
And the glue of your attachments
To each thought, then gives you
Direction, dimension, bulges and crevices.

Emptiness of thought is not real.

Fill the void in your mind.
Take yourself on a journey.

And when that little speck appears,
Get into your rocket ship and net it in,
(Not as debris or waste),
But as a part of the whole.

You must have every aspect of 'you'
Ignited and made come to life
In order to feel alive
And realize that you are indeed
'A LIFE'.

Time

Time does not exist of itself.
It is an illusion;
A perception of reality;
A fragment of your being,
Within a microscopic universe.

It is difficult to portend
What the essence of your being is.

It is merely a condition of the soul,
A practice of your inner being.

What you do is worth more
Than the time you spend doing it.

What you learn from your experiences
Is what time is all about.

For some, the journey seems very long
And for others, there seems to be
No differentiation between
What they do and what they are.

*This is the essence of the message
Of time and being.*

Always spend time being 'who' you are.

*You do not need to prove
Your worth in doing,
Unless the doing
Is part of your being,
And brings you closer
To the light of love, of truth,
And of compassion in all that exists.*

Death is only a portal to the soul.

*At first there is some concern
Of the significance of passing,
But this is all that death is,
A passing on.*

*In life you must endure
That your being passes onto something
Of eternal significance.*

*The smallest deed is often the one
That is of greatest benefit,
For it does not encompass ego
In a way that seems all too relevant
In the human state.*

*Dying in itself, is life's biggest lesson,
For in this process you discover
All that you hold dear.*

*You will discover that
All that lives on eternally,
Is love and that love is all there is.*

*The present is only
The recognition of choice.*

*You must be more deliberate in the choices
That you make rather than dwelling
In the present.*

*How can you live in the present,
When it is a concept that does not exist?*

Live in love.

*Live in worthy choices.
Live with outcomes bathed i
In the glory of essential wonderment,
Trust and goodness.*

*Everything happens as it should,
And your hand does little
To forward the hands of time.*

*All you can do,
Is deliver an ultimatum
On your own perceptions,
And make these into positive
Or negative states of being.*

*Strive for purity in all that you think,
All that you believe,
And all that 'you' are.*

*There is no room for compromise.
There is only room for the clarity
Of a life lived true and full.*

*A calendar is only a reminder
Of the passage of time.*

*This in itself is useful in that
You can be open to change,
Knowing in your heart,
That significant events
Will indeed befall you
And will have an impact
On your being.

You will suffer as with the fall,
And be strengthened by the growth
And the promise of spring.

For everything there is a time,
And morning comes
After each passing day.

There is no prediction necessary.

All that is needed is a firm belief
That whatever the Universe
Determines your fate is to be,
Is exactly what you need
To embrace lovingly,
With light, truth,
Hope and love.*

Trust Yourself

The world as you know it
Is but a mere speck
In the realm of creativity.

Your life but a speck of stardust
But none-the-less paramount
In the purpose of things.

Each crumb is important
For it is food for the birds
That dwell in the night skies.

As a bird does fly,
So too do you need to give flight to
Your own ideas.

Do not rely too heavily
On the thoughts of others.

It is good to have your own basic plan
And from that you must take leaps
And soar into the unknown.

*Confidence is nothing short
Of having belief in yourself.*

*'We' will not see you fail.
But there may be lessons ahead for you
If you decide to choose the way of ego.*

*Stand straight and tall.
Call on us to stand beside you.
Look to us for cues and clues.*

*As long as you are open,
And receptive and do not close up
On your God-given talents, you will achieve.*

*Sow seeds of self-acceptance
In those who have stooped so low
That they look outside of themselves
Instead of within themselves.*

*Show your humanness and your
Ability to err many times.*

*Show your ability to stand strong
In the face of adversity.*

Be strong in yourself.

Be like the willow branch.

Bend and flow with life more.

*Just be 'you' and realise
That you are in 'our' care.
'We' will support and strengthen you
To do and to be all that is necessary.*

Remember to be in the instance only.

*All that is past is past and all that is before you,
Will just unfold as it must.*

*Rely on the knowledge
That lies inert within you.*

*We will bring it forth
If and when you need it.*

*Go in love
And spread that love
As you go.*

Truth

*Heavenly whispers are purely that.
They are whispers from heaven
Of light, of hope, and of truth,
Pure truth, spoken through those
That resonate pure truth.*

*No interpretation must be made
As to the authenticity of truth.*

Truth shall ring out loud and clear for all to hear.

*A joyous sound indeed for those who are in need,
For they will hear the word of their own volition,
Not through a net of garb and jangles
And proclaimed righteousness.*

*Be still, for the sound of truth
Is heard in the wind, the trees and the soil.*

*Earth to earth,
Ashes to ashes,
And life goes on full circle.*

*It is not your quest to fulfil this truth,
For you know it as it is.*

*Your quest is to shed light
Upon the path so that others
May tread more sure-footed and feel
Some illumination, light and guidance.*

*When you are not true to yourself
You will find blockages in your way.*

There is no need to fear truth.

*It is now the right time
To ignore the wants of those
Who are vain in their quest.*

*When you are enticed onto other paths,
Know that this is not for you.*

*You must get back
To your own ideals,
And follow what you know
In your heart to be true for you.*

The truth is not to be questioned,
For it is clear, crystal clear.

When it is the truth,
It makes you stand tall and proud,
And all doubts and fears
Go away and are released.

That is how you will know
What is truth and what is true for' you'.

Doubts do not stand steadfast.

Questions will arise in your soul,
And your demeanour will change
In every perspective as a result.

Avoid looking from side to side.
Instead, face things head on.
Look eye-to-eye and seek the truth therein.

When you cannot see into someone's eyes
And hold their gaze steadfast,
You will know that blockages are there.

Be they yours or theirs is not important.
Just know that you must always
See clear light to proceed.

Honour is not standing by your word,
It is standing by your truth.
Wisdom is not doing what is expected of you,
It is fulfilling your life's purpose.
Openness is not laying yourself bare,
It is saying your truth.
Integrity is only being what 'you' are,
Wholly, fully and intentionally.

Change brings about opportunities,
And the brave are the ones
Who are seekers of the opportunities
That will test their resolve.

Go forward fearlessly.

Do not always lead the way
Because those of a different path
Will need to find their own way.
Tread sure-footed and always leave footprints
For others to follow if they wish.

Unity

A sense of calm must prevail
So that the essence of your being
Can shine and give light to what is within you.

When you do not open up to
What is really going on inside of you,
You will debate facts that are not actually facts,
But are opinions devoid of all the facts.

You always need to clarify. . . .
What are the issues;
What are discussions;
What are opinions;
And what are facts.

You must decipher what is important,
And make this your focus.

To focus on what is not important,
Will lead to reactions
And thoughtlessness in the extreme
In both deed and word.

*Be more deliberate in your actions
And base these on selfless love.*

*The ego does not have a place
In the communion of souls.*

*Why, when you want to reach unity,
Would you avoid all
That melds your hearts together?*

*When you are united in spirit,
You will no longer find discord.*

*But how do you become united
When there is distance and reluctance
On both parts to be bare?*

*There is no easy answer.
Yet the answer is indeed quite simple!*

*First, negate all you do for ego.
Then do only that which is in the name of love.*

All else will fall into place.

*Materialism in itself brings no pleasure.
It is the enjoyment it can bring
To an already full heart that brings you joy.*

*The crosses born in life are indeed heavy loads
Borne by those who can and discarded
By those who cannot see
The value in a life blessed with pain,
And hampered by sorrow.*

*These emotions can only be felt
At the loss of something rich and true,
Something of real value to you.*

*When you are in the thick of grieving,
Know that it is your own inability
To unite freely in love,
That will keep you stuck.*

*Do not lay blame at anyone's feet.
Instead, mend your ways,
And mend your life
To include all that you wish.*

*A heart half full
Is like a fertile crop not harvested.*

*A life not lived to the full
Is like a day without sunset.*

*Ensure each day is full,
Full of love, laughter,
Kindness and love.*

*For this is the way
To live your best life.*

Live forward, not backwards.

*Live your life fully
And with no regrets.*

*Do not concern yourself
With trivialities.*

*The bird does not mind
Where the nectar comes from,
As long as the outcome is sweet.*

USE YOUR GIFTS

Your destiny is just that,
The place that you are meant to be.

However, when we speak of place,
'We' do not mean logistics
Or whereabouts.

'We' speak of the place within the soul,
That radiates out from . . .
A fulfilled life;
A generous heart;
A thoughtful mind;
And a passive resistance to
All of the challenges that lie
In the path of righteousness.

Your way is the way
To the eminent being of your being.

Proclaim all that you are
And be proud of the gifts
Bestowed upon you.

*These gifts are often ignored,
For they seem of little value
In comparison with
Other people's gifts.*

*This is only because
Your gifts lie dormant.*

*A door afraid to be opened,
Will never let the light in,
And will forever shadow what lies inside.*

Open the door to you!

*Peek into the crevices that are illuminated
By the rays of light that shine upon them.*

Ventilate your spirit.

*Open yourself up
To your gifts!*

*Open yourself up
To all 'you' are!*

Be!

Your Garden

*Your soul laid bare is a garden
Ready for planting.*

*The seeds that are sown
Are always a reflection
Of your dreams and anxieties.*

*Your passivity determines the acidity of the soul,
And can burn even the bravest of embryos.*

No decision is fear at its worst.

*A sowing made in faith and pure trust
Will always yield and produce a garden rich and rare.*

*God will always tend the young sapling,
And nourishment will spring forth
From the well of abundant.*

LOVE.

Your Life Is In Your Hands

Your life is mirrored in your hands.

When you reflect on your experiences,
They are not always the way it was.

The gap between reality and your memory of it
Are sometimes quite exaggerated
By your wishes, hopes and perceptions
Of the way you wanted it to be,
Or how you can best explain it
So as to get recognition,
Rather than condemnation.

A life lived fully is not a life lived
Through or for others.

It is a life where the intention
Is always the truth. . .
The truth in 'who' you are
And what 'you' are at
Any and every given moment.

*A life lived for others is nothing short
Of balking out of your own life.*

*You have been given gifts and talents.
These are unique to you,
And must be utilised by you.*

*No one is incomplete.
You all have everything
That you need to be 'you'.*

*When you choose to squander
Or to ignore your God given gifts,
Believing that you are not enough,
You will feel that you are inadequate.*

*Inadequacies occur when
You make comparisons with others,
And your perceptions are that they are
Far greater and better than you.*

*Why then do you not feel over-adequate
With those that you perceive
As less than yourself?*

It is because of your misconstrued ideas
Of what is whole and good.

You are all good no matter what.

Your sense of wholeness
Comes from your acceptance
Of the goodness in 'you'.

It comes from a firm belief in yourself
And that all you need
Is to be 'yourself'.

That is enough.

It is so silly really to try
To emulate another
When you can only be yourself.

You are all unique individuals.
This is what makes
Each one of 'you' so special.

Self-love is nourishment
To the soul.

Your Time On Earth

When you are born, your journey of
The mortal commences.

This is a time of learning,
And glimpsing the portals of your soul,
Till you are at one,
Once again with God.

On the eternal plane,
The universe is vast
And incomprehensible
To the human mind.

The child comes into the world
Free in his mind,
For he has nought but himself
And his basic needs
To occupy his thoughts.

As he grows into his human form,
He learns the consequences
Of free will and choice.

*For each choice there is another one
Just around the corner.*

*Each and every choice
Has far reaching effects,
Not only on yourself,
But on others as well.*

*It is just as important
To make so-called wrong choices,
As it is to choose the expected.*

*This is how your lives
Become meandering tracks,
Instead of safe, secure
And dull existences.*

*You must stray on occasions,
In order to feel that
You have chosen correctly.
You cannot make a choice,
If you do not know the options
And the consequences thereof.*

Life must be treated as an adventure.

*You are here on this earth
To take risks, to test your limits
And to do more than just survive.*

*You are here to partake
In the immenseness of this world
You have chosen to experience.*

*You must not be content
In following the footprints of another.*

*You must fathom your depths
And reach beyond your limitations.*

*Seek relentlessly
For that which you call
God, peace, light, love and harmony.*

*Just as the colours of the rainbow
Light up the skies after
Torrential rains and storms,
So too must you illuminate
All your inner qualities,
In harmony with each other,
And in harmony with life.*

To Be Remembered

To be remembered is to leave
An indelible impression on someone
Whose heart, mind and very soul
Has been touched by you.

Material things are transient.
Money never lasts very long.
Promises not kept become defaults.
And a life lived in selfishness,
Is just a disaster in the end.

It is often the smallest things,
That leave the biggest indentation
. . . The ripple effect

It is our virtues that people remember.
And the virtues 'we' speak of
Are Faith, Hope and Charity.

To give someone a lifeline,
When they are bereft
And without an anchor.

To show someone a light,
When darkness has overshadowed them.

To give of yourself and to give freely,
With no thought of recompense.

These, which add up to love,
Are what we are remembered for.

To leave a legacy is just like
Leaving a footprint in the sand.

The tides and time wash them away.

But when you leave an indelible footprint
On the heart, soul to soul,
It lasts forever.

'We' believe that if you
Are remembered for love,
Then you will be remembered
For the greatest of all qualities.

Because it's love,
That oils the wheels of human joy.

Conclusion

To say that this is the end
Of 'our' communications,
Would be to say that
The ship has now sailed.

And when it is time
For the anchor to be lowered,
'We' will once again be there
To provide more earth beneath your feet.

We wish the following for you:

* To see with your eyes wide open.

* To sing in praise of all of your abundant gifts.

* To fill your heart till it overflows
With unconditional love.

Fill your world that is so in need:
With a kind word, a gentle caress
And a loving spirit.

Our words will not be in vain,
For they will find their resting place
In so many hearts that are lost and open
To the truth written herein.

There does come a time when each sparrow
Must take flight... And fly you must.

Test your wings and know always,
That love resides in a pure heart.

Above all do not hold
Any malice towards another.

Love freely and often.
To find riches far beyond
Your wildest imaginings.

Live your life true,
And believe in the 'you'
That has been created.

This is all 'we' ask.

Utilise all your gifts and look to others
For that which is lacking.

Then go and fulfil the good
In, and of, all mankind.

Band together as brothers.
Allow vulnerability to strengthen you.

Allow emptiness to provide you
With the vessel to receive abundance.

Allow these words to penetrate
Your thoughts and your actions,
In order that you may fulfil your dreams
As well as your passions.

If you reach your own goals
As well as those set for you,
You will honour your existence
And your purpose for living.

* * *

Pay it Forward

Whether you received 'Emails From Heaven' as a gift, borrowed it from a friend, or purchased it yourself, I'm so glad you read it and I hope you continue to read it and find inspiration from it in the future.

In my own life, it has come as such a blessing, and the words have been a guide as well as a reminder to value 'myself' as well as the gift that is 'my life'.

When something this profound comes to you and changes you and your life for the better, you need to pay it forward.

So, please share the words, the thoughts and messages in your 'Emails From Heaven' with your family and friends.

If you are interested in writing to me, sharing your experiences and the blessings and miracles that have happened in your life as a direct result of your 'Emails From Heaven',

Or if you would like more information about my upcoming Shows or Workshops and anything else I'm working on

Or you would like me to speak at an event you are hosting

Please contact me as I would love to hear from you.

Maya

Maya Knight

PO Box 179
Bulahdelah NSW 2423 Australia

Phone: +61 (0) 413305001

Website: www.mayapalmist.com

Email: maya.palmist@gmail.com

www.ingramcontent.com/pod-product-compliance
Lightning Source LLC
Chambersburg PA
CBHW050310010526
44107CB00055B/2184